COUNTRIES

Russia

Alice Harman

WAYLAND

Explore the world with **Popcorn -** your complete first non-fiction library.

Look out for more titles in the Popcorn range. All books have the same format of simple text and striking images. Text is carefully matched to the pictures to help readers to identify and understand key vocabulary. www.waylandbooks.co.uk/popcorn

First published in 2012 by Wayland
Copyright © Wayland 2012

Wayland
Hachette Children's Books
338 Euston Road
London NW1 3BH

Wayland Australia
Level 17/207 Kent Street
Sydney NSW 2000

Produced for Wayland by
White-Thomson Publishing Ltd
www.wtpub.co.uk
+44 (0)843 208 7460

Editor: Alice Harman
Designer: Clare Nicholas
Picture researcher: Alice Harman
Series consultant: Kate Ruttle
Design concept: Paul Cherrill

British Library Cataloging in Publication Data
Harman, Alice
   Russia. -- (Countries)(Popcorn)
   1. Russia (Federation)--Juvenile literature.
   I. Title II. Series
   914.7-dc23

ISBN: 978 0 7502 6743 4

Wayland is a division of Hachette Children's Books,
an Hachette UK company.
www.hachette.co.uk

Printed and bound in China

Picture/Illustration Credits: Alamy: Losevsky Pavel 8, frans lemmens 15; Peter Bull 23; Stefan Chabluk 4; Dreamstime: Tomi Tenetz 5, Irakite 16tr, Jjspring 17, Mikhail Olykainen 21; Shutterstock: Anna Miller 6, Maxim Tupikov 7, withGod 9, swinner 10, Fedor A. Sidorov 11, yui 12, Solodovnikova Elena 13, Lucertolone 14, Kokhanchikov 16br, Andrey Starostin 16bl, Govorov Pavel 18, ermess 19, De Visu 20

Every effort has been made to clear copyright. Should there be any inadvertent omission, please apply to the publisher for rectification.

 Contents

Where is Russia?

Here is a map of Russia. Russia is
the biggest country in the world.
Some of Russia is in Europe,
and some is in Asia.

Moscow is the capital of Russia. It is in the west of the country. Moscow is the biggest city in Europe, and the sixth largest city in the world.

The Kremlin, in Moscow's Red Square, is where the Russian president lives.

Land and sea

There are long, high mountain ranges in Russia, but most of the country is flat grassland. Northern Russia has huge areas of forest, and frozen land called tundra.

Mount Elbrus, in southern Russia, is the highest mountain in Europe.

Nearly a quarter of all the world's forest is in Russia.

Russia has the longest coastline in the world. Its coast runs along parts of two oceans and four seas.

In the sea along Russia's eastern coast, there are huge rocks covered with pine trees.

The weather

In summer, most of the country is quite warm. It is colder in the north than in the south. There is sometimes very hot weather in southern Russia.

Lots of Russians come to enjoy the sun on Anapa's long, sandy beaches.

Winters in Russia are normally long and cold. In northern Russia, snow and frost covers the land for months.

Many lakes freeze over in winter, and people go ice fishing.

North Siberia is the coldest place in the world where people live.

Town and country

Most Russian people live in cities and towns. Moscow and St Petersburg are the biggest cities in Russia.

The centre of Moscow has tall, new office buildings made of glass and steel.

There are many thousands of villages all over Russia. Most people who live in villages work on farms. They often grow their own food.

Russian villages are normally very small, with fewer than 200 people.

Homes

In the countryside, there are traditional old houses built of wood. Newer houses are normally larger, and stay warmer in winter.

In summer, people come to stay in the wooden houses on the edge of Lake Baikal.

Russian families in cities often have summer houses in the countryside.

In big cities such as Moscow, many people live in tall blocks of flats. Hundreds of people can live in one building.

Most houses in Moscow are less than 40 years old.

Shopping

Some towns and cities in Russia have large stores that sell gifts and luxury goods. These stores are normally in the centre of town.

Around New Year's Eve, lots of stores put up lights and decorations.

People shop in markets for food, clothes and other goods. It is normally cheaper to shop here than in large stores.

The food markets in St Petersburg get very busy at the weekend.

There are more than 3,500 markets in Russia.

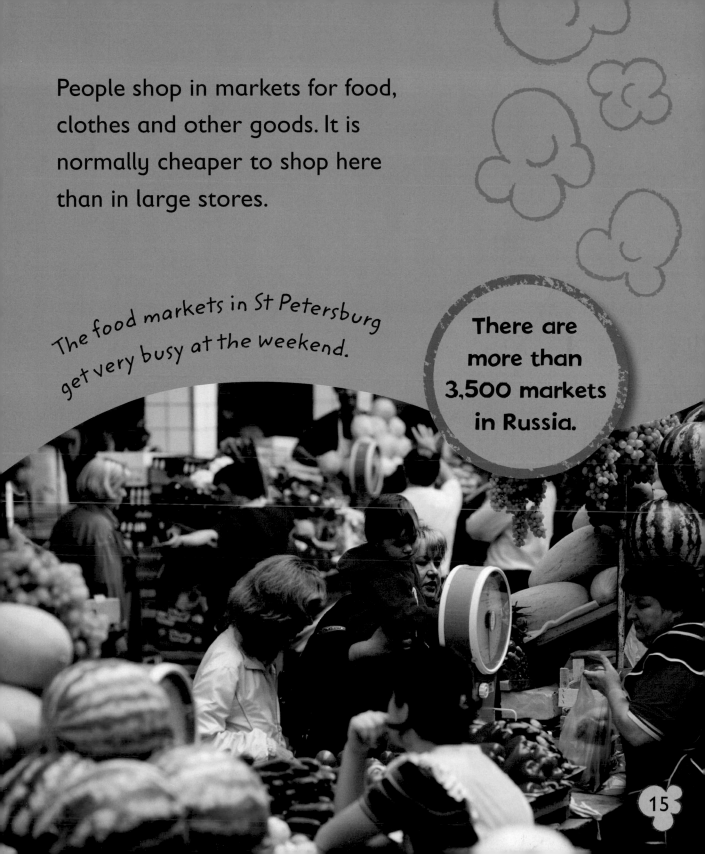

Food

Soups, pies and meat dishes are popular in Russia. Vegetables such as beetroot, cabbage and potato are eaten in salads and cooked meals.

Borscht is a soup made with beetroot, beef and onion.

Thin pancakes, called blintzes, are often eaten with honey or jam.

Russian dumplings are called pelmeni. They are normally filled with meat, fish or mushrooms.

Most Russian towns and cities have lots of kiosks selling hot, cheap street food. Filled pancakes and pastries are traditional Russian street foods.

Pizza slices and hot dogs are popular street foods in Russia.

Sport and leisure

Ice hockey, gymnastics and football are all popular in Russia. Teams often win international prizes in these sports.

Russia has its own martial art, called sambo.

Ice hockey can be dangerous, so players wear helmets to stay safe.

Lots of Russians enjoy folk dancing and ballet. The Bolshoi Ballet group in Moscow is famous. Its dancers perform all over the world.

Different areas of Russia each have their own traditional folk dances.

Holidays and festivals

Russia Day is celebrated on 12 June. It is a national holiday in Russia, so people don't have to work or go to school.

On Russia Day, some people wear traditional clothes and eat homemade cakes.

In Russia, Christmas is celebrated on 7 January. The night before, families eat a meal of 12 dishes called 'The Holy Supper'.

Grandfather Frost and the Snow Maiden give gifts to children all over Russia on New Year's Eve.

Speak Russian!

Russian is the fourth most spoken language in the world. The sounds that make up some Russian words are written below.

Dar	Yes
Nyet	No
Par-jar-list-ar	Please
Spa-see-bar	Thank you
Zdras-twich-yeh	Hello
Dus vi-dan-yuh	Goodbye
Meen-yar-zar goot…	My name is…

The white stripe on the flag stands for peace and honesty. The blue is for loyalty and the red is for energy.

Make Russian dolls

You will need:
- White paper
- Black pen · Colouring pencils
- Scissors · Sticky tape

Russian dolls are traditionally made out of wood and painted in bright colours. They show a woman wearing a headscarf and a patterned dress.

1. Copy the shape of these dolls in black pen. Draw patterns on your doll's dress.

2. Colour your doll in with bright colours, and cut it out.

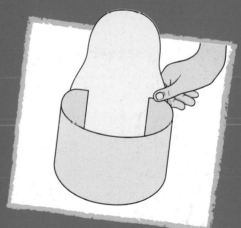

3. Cut out a strip of paper, about half as tall as the doll. Curve it round and stick each end to the back of your doll.

4. Your doll can stand up by itself! Make more dolls, big and small, to build a nice family.

Visit our website to download larger, printable templates for this project.
www.waylandbooks.co.uk/popcorn

23

Glossary

ballet a type of dance performed to music

capital the city where the government of the country meets

department store a large store with different sections for toys, clothes, food and other goods

frost a thin covering of ice

ice fishing trying to catch fish through a hole cut in the ice to the water below

international to do with two or more different countries

kiosk a small stall that normally sells food or newspapers

luxury something that is pleasant but not necessary

martial art an activity based on defending yourself when someone is trying to hurt you

New Year's Eve the night of 31 January

president the leader of the government, in some countries

steel a hard, very strong metal

Index

EXPLORE THE WORLD WITH THE POPCORN NON-FICTION LIBRARY!

- Develops children's knowledge and understanding of the world by covering a wide range of topics in a fun, colourful and engaging way
- Simple sentence structure builds readers' confidence
- Text checked by an experienced literacy consultant and primary deputy-head teacher
- Closely matched pictures and text enable children to decode words
- Includes a cross-curricular activity in the back of each book

WATCH OUT! — Near Water — *Honor Head*

HISTORY CORNER — The Great Fire of London — *Jenny Powell*

SCIENCE CORNER — Sound and Hearing — *Angela Royston*

FAMILIES — My Mum — *Katie Dicker*

GOOD FOOD — Vegetables — *Julia Adams*

PEOPLE WHO HELP US — Police — *Honor Head*

PEOPLE WHO HELP US — Firefighters — *Honor Head*

GEOGRAPHY CORNER — Rainforests — *Ruth Thomson*

A YEAR OF FESTIVALS — Muslim Festivals — *Honor Head*

HISTORY CORNER — The Gunpowder Plot — *Jenny Powell*

IN SPACE — Planets — *Chris Oxlade*

SEASONS — Winter — *Kay Barnham*

FREE DOWNLOADS!

- Written by an experienced teacher
- Learning objectives clearly marked
- Provides information on where the books fit into the curriculum
- Photocopiable so pupils can take them home

OVER 50 TITLES TO CHOOSE FROM!

www.waylandbooks.co.uk/downloads